JAVA JAMBOREE: A WEEKLONG ADVENTURE INTO PROGRAMMING EXCELLENCE

2

Contents

3

4

First day. Start of Java?

Java: What's happening here?

Sun Microsystems made the obvious level, adaptable, and object-arranged programming language known as Java during the 1990s. Since Java programs are stage autonomous, they can run on any gadget that has the Java Virtual Machine (JVM) introduced. Java is sensible for countless usages, from cells to large business level servers, in view of its "make once, run wherever" incorporate.

Key Highlights of Java:

Stage Autonomy: Bytecode is the widely appealing kind of Java code that can be executed on any device with a JVM. This advances cross-stage similarity.

Object-Oriented: Java notices the rules of article coordinated programming (OOP), which incorporates contemplations like portrayal, legacy, and polymorphism. This improves reusability and code affiliation.

The chiefs' altered memories: Java utilizes a trash master to regularly direct memory, lessening the probability of memory breaks and making memory the board more strong for organizers.

Rich Standard Library: Java's wide standard library saves engineers time and effort by giving pre-collected value to ordinary endeavors.

Support for Multithreading: Java certainly upholds multithreading, permitting designers to make simultaneous and equivalent applications.

Security: Systems are safeguarded from malignant code by Java's hearty security model. Applets, a piece of Java, were once widely used to safely additionally foster web information.

Setting Up the Java Progress Climate:

You must set up your progression environment before you can begin programming in Java. These are the crucial stages:

Download and Introduce JDK (Java Movement Pack):

Visit the Prophet JDK or OpenJDK site to download the most recent variety of the JDK.

Follow the establishment rules for your working construction.

Select a Code Manager or Coordination of Progress Climate (IDE):

Notable decisions merge IntelliJ Thought, Obscuration, and Visual Studio Code.

Plan to use the JDK you presented with your chosen IDE.

Create the most important Java program you can:

Open your code boss/IDE and make another Java class.

Fundamentally express "Hello there, World!" test your game plan with a program.

```
System.out.println("Hello, World!");
```
Java Duplicate the code in the public static void main(String[] args) from the public class HelloWorld.

```
    }
}
```

Arrange and Run:

Utilize the solicitation line or the IDE's sure gadgets to hoard and run your program.

Major Improvement of a Java Program:

A Java program conventionally includes something like one classes. An initial development is as follows:

java Copy code//A Java class public class MyClass//The program's primary methodology is at the program's entry point public static void main(String[] args)//The

```
program's thinking goes here
System.out.println("Hello, Java!");
    }
}
```

This is an irrelevant "Hello, Java!" program. You'll learn about factors, data types, control stream, and thing arranged programming thoughts sooner rather than later.

An Outline of Programming: What is Redoing?

The most common method of planning and building an executable PC program to complete a task or resolve a problem is through the writing of computer programs. It involves composing a bunch of guidelines that a PC can fathom and do in a programming language. These guidelines are referred to as code, and the process of writing computer programs basically teaches the computer how to carry out a particular task. Programming engages computerization, computation, and the arrangement of programming applications that power numerous devices and systems.

Programming incorporates a couple of key thoughts:

- Algorithm: a set of rules or instructions that are broken down step by step in order to solve a particular problem or finish a task.

- Variables: Limit regions that hold data values. Elements can change during the execution of a program.

- Control Process: The solicitation wherein headings are executed. This integrates conditions (if decrees), circles, and spreading.

- Data Structures: Trees, records, and clusters are instances of information association and capacity techniques.

- Functions/Methods: reusable blocks of code that carry out a particular task. Functions help modularize code in order to make it easier to read and maintain.

An Overview of Java and Its Functions:

Java:

Java is a significant level, universally useful programming language made to deal with any stage. In the 1990s, Sun Microsystems, which is presently claimed by Prophet, created it. Java applications are consolidated to bytecode, which can run on any device with a Java Virtual Machine (JVM). This key component makes Java a notable choice for building cross-stage applications.

Key Characteristics of Java:

Create Once, Run Wherever (WORA): With a functioning JVM, Java code can be written on one platform and run on another.

Object-Oriented: Java is an article arranged programming (OOP) language that stresses the association and reuse of code using classes and items.

Solid and Secure: Java's strong sort checking part finds botches during collection, and its security features make it sensible for building secure applications.

Rich Standard Library: Java goes with a broad standard library that gives pre-built convenience to ordinary endeavors, diminishing the necessity for creators to make code without any planning.

Uses of Java:

Web Headway: Java is used to collect server-side applications and dynamic web content using headways like Servlets, JSP (JavaServer Pages), and Spring.

Adventure Applications: Java is frequently used to build large-scale project applications, such as customer relationship management (CRM) frameworks and human resources management systems (HRMS), to name just a few.

Convenient Applications: Java (or Kotlin, one more programming language that sudden spikes in demand for the Java Virtual Machine) is regularly utilized in the making of Android applications.

Software for the PC: Java Swing and JavaFX structures are used to make graphical UIs for workspace applications.

Incorporated Frameworks: Java is used in embedded structures for various devices and mechanical assemblies.

Enormous Data and Conveyed figuring: Java is used in colossal data taking care of designs (e.g., Apache Hadoop) and disseminated figuring stages.

Understanding the basics of programming and Java gives major areas of strength for a to bouncing further into the language and its applications. As you progress, you'll research subjects, for instance, factors, data types, control stream, and article organized programming in Java.

Downloading and Introducing the Java Advancement Pack (JDK):

Step 1: Pick a JDK Circulation:

Visit the authority Prophet JDK site or the OpenJDK site to download the JDK appropriation.

Prophet JDK: OpenJDK is downloaded by Oracle JDK: OpenJDK Downloads

Stage 2: Download and Run the Installer:

Select the suitable JDK adaptation for your working framework (Windows, macOS, or Linux).

Download the installer executable.

Run the installer and adhere to the establishment guidelines gave.

Step 3: Verify the setup:

When the establishment is finished, open an order brief (Windows) or a terminal (macOS/Linux) and type the accompanying order to confirm that Java has been introduced:

slam
Duplicate code
java - rendition
This ought to show data about the introduced Java variant.

Step 4: Set the JAVA_HOME Climate Variable (Discretionary):
Setting the JAVA_HOME climate variable can be valuable for specific advancement apparatuses. You can set it to the establishment registry of your JDK. On Windows, for instance:

Windows:

"Advanced system settings" will appear.
Click on the "Climate Factors" button.
Under "Framework Factors," click "New" and add a variable named JAVA_HOME with the way to your JDK establishment (e.g., C:\Program Files\Java\jdk1.8.0_301).
Click "Alright" to close the windows.

Configuring a Code Editor:

IntelliJ Thought:
Download and Introduce IntelliJ Thought:

Visit the IntelliJ Thought site and download the Local area or Extreme version.
Run the installer and adhere to the establishment guidelines.
Open IntelliJ Thought:

Open IntelliJ IDEA following installation.
Set up your advancement climate by arranging the JDK:
Select "Project Structure" under "File."
Under "Task," set the "Venture SDK" to the JDK you introduced.
Click "Alright" to save the settings.
Eclipse:

Eclipse: Download and install it.

Visit the Shroud Downloads page and download the Overshadowing IDE for Java Engineers.
Run the installer and adhere to the establishment guidelines.
Open Obscuration:

After establishment, open Obscuration.
Set up the JDK:
Go to "Window" > "Inclinations."
Explore to "Java" > "Introduced JREs."
Click "Add External JARs" and select the tools.jar in the lib folder of your installed JDK to add it.
Visual Studio Code:

Download and Introduce Visual Studio Code:

Visit the Visual Studio Code site and download the installer.
Run the installer and adhere to the establishment directions.

Introduce Java Augmentation Pack:

Open Visual Studio Code.
Go to the Expansions view by tapping on the Augmentations symbol in the Movement Bar on the window or press Ctrl+Shift+X.
Look for "Java Expansion Pack" and introduce it.

Arrange JDK in Visual Studio Code:

Open a Java document or make another one.
Whenever provoked, introduce the suggested augmentations.

You might see a prompt to set up the Java Development Kit (JDK) in the bottom-right corner. Click on it and select the introduced JDK.

Presently, you've effectively set up your Java improvement climate with a code proofreader of your decision. You can begin composing and running Java code in your chose manager.

You're Most memorable Java Program:

We should make a straightforward "Hi, World!" program in Java. This exemplary model is utilized to show the essential punctuation and design of a Java program.

Step 1: Open Your Code Supervisor:

Open your favored code supervisor (e.g., IntelliJ Thought, Obscuration, Visual Studio Code).

Step 2: Make Another Java Class:

In Java, the code is coordinated into classes. A class is an outline for objects. For our "Hi, World!" program, we should make a class named HelloWorld.

In IntelliJ Thought:

Go to "Document" > "New" > "Java Class."

Enter HelloWorld as the Class Name.

Actually look at the container that says "public static void main(String[] args)."

Click "Alright" to make the class.

With Eclipse,

Go to "Document" > "New" > "Class."

Enter HelloWorld as the Name of the class.

Actually look at the crate that says "public static void main(String[] args)."

Click "Finish" to make the class.

In Visual Studio Code:

Make another record and save it with the name HelloWorld.java.

Inside the document, enter the accompanying code:

java

Duplicate code

```java
public class HelloWorld {

    // Code for your program goes here
  }
}
```

Stage 3: Write "Hello, World!" down. Code:

Inside the principal strategy, compose the accompanying code to print "Hi, World!" to the display:

java
Duplicate code

```java
public class HelloWorld {

    System.out.println("Hello, World!");
  }
}
```

Step 4: Run the Program:

Presently, you're prepared to run your most memorable Java program.

In IntelliJ Thought or Obscuration: Right-click on the record containing the primary strategy (HelloWorld.java).

Select "Run" or "Run As" > "Java Application."

In Visual Studio Code, this:

Open the terminal.

Go to the folder where your HelloWorld.java file is stored.

Order the code utilizing the order:

javac HelloWorld.java

Run the aggregated program with:

java HelloWorld

Stage 5: View Result:

You ought to see the result "Hi, World!" printed to the control center. Congratulations! Your first Java program has been written and executed successfully.

Understanding the Essential Design of a Java Program:

Presently, how about we separate the essential construction of the program:

Class Statement: The declaration of the HelloWorld class marks the beginning of the program. Every Java application needs at least one class.

primary Technique: The fundamental technique is the section point of a Java program. The strategy gets executed when the program begins running. In our model, it prints "Hi, World!" the System.out.println statement to the console.

Comments: Remarks in Java start with//for single-line remarks or/* to begin a block of remarks and */to end it. Remarks are not executed and are utilized to give clarifications and documentation.

As you progress into more advanced Java programming concepts, having a solid understanding of these fundamental elements is essential. Feel free to play around with the code and discover additional Java language and code editor features.

Day 2: Welcome to Day 2 of your journey to learn Java

Java Stray pieces!

Today, we will dive into two or three fundamental contemplations of Java programming that will furnish you with a solid planning. We should analyze factors, information types, administrators, and control stream clarifications.

4. Factors and Information Types:

4.1 Components:

In Java, a variable is a breaking point locale that holds information. It looks like a named compartment for taking care of characteristics, to you.

java
Duplicate code
public class VariablesExample {

```
    // Pronounce factors
    int age;
    twofold level;

    // Assign values to age = 25
factors;
    level = 5.9;

    // System.out.println("Age: ")
produces values. + age);
    System.out.println("Height: " +
level);
  }
}
```

4.2 Information Types:

Unrefined and reference types are two of Java's inborn data types. Raw sorts merge int, twofold, burn, and boolean.

java
Duplicate code

```java
public class DataTypesExample {

    // Raw information types
    int intValue = 42;
    twofold doubleValue = 3.14;
    burn charValue = 'A';
    boolean Value is significant;

    // Print values
    System.out.println("Int   Worth:
" + valueInteger);
    "Twofold        Worth:"        =
doubleValue,     system.out.println,
and
    System.out.println("Char
Worth: " + charValue);
    System.out.println("Boolean
Worth: " + boolean esteem);
  }
}
```

5. Operators:

5.1 Computing Chiefs:

Number rearranging heads perform basic numerical activities.

java Copy the int a = 10, b = 5 code;

```
"Sum:" = system.out.println + (a + b));
    "Qualification:                    ",
system.out.println, + (a - b));
```

Officials in charge of social control:
Social chiefs are utilized to contemplate values.

java copy code: public static void main(String[] args) int x = 5, y = 10; public class RelationalOperatorsExample

```
"Is x identical to y?" receives its return from system.out.println. + (x == y));
```

"Is x not comparable to y?" is printed by system.out.println. + (x ! = y));
"Is x more significant than y?" receives its return from system.out.println. + (x > y));
System.out.println("Is x not exactly or indistinguishable from y? " + (x <= y));
   }
}

6.   Stream   of   Control Articulations:

6.1 If Explanation:

The assuming that statement licenses you to execute a block of code given that a destined condition is significant.

java

Duplicate code

public class IfStatementExample {

```java
        int number = 7;

    if (number % 2 == 0) {
        System.out.println("The number is even.");
    } else {
        System.out.println("The number is odd.");
    }
  }
}
```

6.2 Switch Statement:

The switch explanation awards you to pick one of many code blocks to be executed.

java Copy the public class SwitchStatementExample's code with the following:

day of the week, case 1 of the switch:

```java
System.out.println("Monday");
        break;
    case 2:
```

```java
System.out.println("Tuesday");
        break;
    // Add additional cases for additional days obviously:
        System.out.println("Invalid day");
```

6.3 Loops: for, while, and do-while

You can run a block of code again and again using circles.

Java copy code for LoopsExample:

```java
public static void main(String[] args)//For circle for (int I = 1; i <= 5; i++) {
        System.out.println("Iteration " + I);
    }
```

```java
// While circle
int j = 1;
while (j <= 5) {
    System.out.println("Iteration " + j);
    j++;
}

// Do-while circle
int k = 1;
do {
    System.out.println("Iteration " + k);
    k++;
} while (k <= 5);
```

Congrats on finishing Day 2! These contemplations are head to Java programming, and overpowering them will plan for extra made subjects. Work on making code, research different streets as for various conditions,

and go ahead and ask expecting you
have any solicitations!

Overseers of Java:

Math Heads:

Number modifying heads perform essential mathematical exercises.

```java
Copy code
public                                    class
ArithmeticOperatorsExample {

    int a = 10, b = 5;

    "Sum:" = system.out.println + (a
+ b));
    "Capability:                          ",
system.out.println, + (a - b));
    System.out.println("Product:    "
+ (a * b));
    System.out.println("Quotient:   "
+ (a / b));
    System.out.println("Remainder:
" + (a % b));
```

Supervising Social Workers: Social bosses are used to consider values.

Java code copying: public static void main(String[] args) int x = 5, y = 10; public class RelationalOperatorsExample

```
    "Is x indistinguishable from y?" accepts its return from system.out.println. + (x == y));
    "Is x not equivalent to y?" is printed by system.out.println. + (x ! = y));
    "Is x more critical than y?" accepts its return from system.out.println. + (x > y));
    System.out.println("Is x not precisely or indistinct from y? " + (x <= y));
  }
}
```

Steady Chairmen:

On boolean attributes, trustworthy chiefs follow fitting strategies.

```java
java public static void main(String[]
args) boolean a = real, b = misled;
System.out.println("Logical AND: "):
public static void main(String[]
args). + (a && b));
    "Then again cleverly:  "  =
system.out.println + (a || b));
    System.out.println("Logical
NOT: " + ! a);
  }
}
```

Getting a handle on Executive Need:

Manager need concludes the evaluation solicitation of an enunciation's chairmen. Priority is given to supervisors with greater demands.

```java
Copy code
public class OperatorPrecedenceExample {

    int result = 5 * 3 + 8/2;
    System.out.println("Result: " + result);
```

In the preceding model, increment is examined first because it has a greater need than expansion and division.

Control Stream Clarifications:

In the event of confirmation:
The expecting validation licenses prohibitive execution of code.

```java
Copy code
public class IfStatementExample {

    int number = 7;
```

```java
    if (number % 2 == 0) {
        System.out.println("The number is even.");
    } else {
        System.out.println("The number is odd.");
```

Switch syllable articulation:
The switch clarification grants you to pick one of many code blocks to be executed.

java
Copy code

```java
public class SwitchStatementExample {

    int dayOfWeek = 3;
```

day of the week, case 1 of the switch:

```java
System.out.println("Monday");
```

```java
        break;
    case 2:

System.out.println("Tuesday");
        break;
        // Add extra cases for extra days clearly:
        System.out.println("Invalid day");
```

Circles (for, while, and do-while):

For Circle:

The for circle grants you to feature a block of code a destined number of times.

java
Copy code
```java
public class ForLoopExample {

    for (int I = 1; i <= 5; i++) {
        System.out.println("Iteration " + I);
```

```
        }
      }
}
```

While Circle:

When a particular condition proves to be true, the while circle repeats a block of code.

With int j comparable to 1, the public class WhileLoopExample in Java was duplicated from the public static void main(String[] args).

```
    while (j <= 5) {
        System.out.println("Iteration " + j);
        j++;
    }
  }
}
```

Do-While Circle:

The do-while circle is like the while circle regardless ensures that the block of code is executed some spot close once.

DoWhileLoopExample.java is a copy of the public static void main(String[] args) int k = 1;

```
    do {
        System.out.println("Iteration " + k);
        k++;
    } while (k <= 5);
```

I'm thankful! You've covered number improving, social, and reasonable bosses, as well as control stream clarifications. The pivotal design blocks for more confounded and dynamic Java programs are these. To improve your discernment, work on framing code and researching various streets as for various conditions. Please feel free to make any requests you might have!

Day 3: Object-Arranged Programming (OOP) Essentials

Welcome to Day 3 of your Java learning venture! Today, we'll investigate the basic ideas of Item Arranged Programming (OOP) in Java. Object-situated writing computer programs is a worldview that spins around the idea of items, which can exemplify information and conduct. How about we plunge into the key ideas:

7. Prologue to Articles and Classes:

7.1 Items:

Objects are occasions of classes and address genuine elements with ascribes (information) and ways of behaving (techniques).

They epitomize information and conduct, giving a method for

organizing and model complex frameworks.

7.2 Classes:

Classes are outlines or layouts for making objects.

They specify the class's object structure, including its attributes and methods.

8. Characterizing Classes and Making Articles:

8.1 Class Announcement:

A class is pronounced utilizing the class catchphrase followed by the class name.

Fields (traits) and strategies are characterized inside the class.

java Copy code for the public class Car; // Fields String brand;

```
    String model;
    int year;

    // Techniques
    void startEngine() {
```

```java
    System.out.println("Engine started!");
  }

  void speed up() {

System.out.println("Accelerating...");
```

8.2 Constructing Objects:
Objects are made utilizing the new watchword followed by the class constructor.

java
Duplicate code
```java
public class ObjectCreationExample {

    // Make objects of the Vehicle class
    Vehicle myCar = new Vehicle();
    Vehicle anotherCar = new Vehicle();
```

```java
    // Getting to protest fields and strategies
    myCar.brand = "Toyota";
    myCar.model must be "Camry";
    myCar.year = 2022;

    "My car: ", System.out.println("
+ myCar.brand + " " + myCar.model
+ " " + myCar.year);
    myCar.startEngine();
    myCar.accelerate();

    // ... make and collaborate with anotherCar
  }
}
```

9. Inheritance:

9.1 Broadening Classes:

Legacy permits a class (subclass) to acquire the qualities and techniques for another class (superclass).

It advances code reuse and upholds the "is-a" relationship.

java
Duplicate code

```java
public class SportsCar broadens Vehicle {
    // Extra fields and techniques well defined for SportsCar
    boolean super;

    void engageTurbo() {
        super = valid;
        System.out.println("Turbo engaged!");
    }
}
```

10. Polymorphism:

10.1 Technique Over-burdening:

Technique over-burdening permits a class to have various strategies with a similar name however unique boundary records.

java
Duplicate code

```java
public class MathOperations {
```

```java
    // Strategy over-burdening
    int add(int a, int b) {
        return a + b;
    }

    twofold add(double a, twofold b)
{
        return a + b;
    }
}
```

10.2 Strategy Superseding:

Strategy superseding happens when a subclass gives a particular execution to a technique characterized in its superclass.

java

Duplicate code

```java
public class Creature {
    void makeSound() {
        System.out.println("Some
conventional sound");
    }
}
```

```
public class Canine expands Creature {
    // Strategy abrogating
    void makeSound() {
        System.out.println("Woof! Woof!");
```

The Bottom Line:

Object-arranged programming includes the utilization of articles and classes to demonstrate and structure code.

Classes are the blueprints that are used to create objects that have behaviors (methods) and attributes (fields).

Legacy permits a class to acquire the properties of another class, advancing code reuse.

Method overloading and method overriding are both made possible by polymorphism.

Investigate these ideas further through active practice. Make your classes, try different things with legacy, and notice polymorphic way of behaving. Understanding OOP is urgent for building versatile and secluded Java applications.

Prologue to Articles and Classes:

1. Objects:

Objects are examples of classes and address genuine elements.

They contain both behavior (methods) and data (attributes).

2. Classes:

Classes are outlines or layouts for making objects.

They characterize the design and conduct that objects of the class will have.

Characterizing Classes and Making Items:

3. Class Announcement:

A class is proclaimed utilizing the class watchword, trailed by the class name.

Fields (traits) and strategies are characterized inside the class.

java Copy code for the public class Car; // Fields String brand;

String model;

```java
    int year;

    // Techniques
    void startEngine() {
        System.out.println("Engine started!");
    }

    void speed up() {

System.out.println("Accelerating...")
;
    }
}
```

4. Making Items:

Objects are made utilizing the new watchword followed by the class constructor.

java

Duplicate code

public class ObjectCreationExample
{

```java
    // Make objects of the Vehicle class
    Vehicle myCar = new Vehicle();
    Vehicle anotherCar = new Vehicle();

    // Getting to protest fields and strategies
    myCar.brand = "Toyota";
    myCar.model must be "Camry";
    myCar.year = 2022;

    "My car: ", System.out.println("
+ myCar.brand + " " + myCar.model
+ " " + myCar.year);
    myCar.startEngine();
    myCar.accelerate();

    // ... make and collaborate with anotherCar
  }
}
```

Constructors and Strategies:

5. Constructors:

When an object is created, special methods called constructors are used to initialize its state.

They have a similar name as the class and don't have a bring type back.

java Copy code for the public class Car; // Fields String brand;

```java
    String model;
    int year;

    // Constructor
    public Car(String brand, String model, int year) {
        this.brand = brand;
        this.model = model;
        this is the year;
    }

    // Strategies
    void startEngine() {
```

```java
        System.out.println("Engine started!");
    }

    void speed up() {

System.out.println("Accelerating...");
    inherited wealth:
```

6. Broadening Classes:

Legacy permits a class (subclass) to acquire the qualities and techniques for another class (superclass).

java

Duplicate code

```java
public class SportsCar broadens Vehicle {
    // Extra fields and techniques well defined for SportsCar
    boolean super;

    void engageTurbo() {
        super = valid;
```

```java
        System.out.println("Turbo engaged!");
    }
}
```

7. Abrogating Strategies:

Strategy superseding happens when a subclass gives a particular execution to a technique characterized in its superclass.

java

Duplicate code

```java
public class Creature {
    void makeSound() {
        System.out.println("Some conventional sound");
    }
}


public class Canine expands Creature {
    // Strategy abrogating
    void makeSound() {
```

```java
        System.out.println("Woof! Woof!");
    }
}
```

Polymorphism:

8. Strategy Over-burdening and Superseding:

Strategy Over-burdening: Numerous strategies with a similar name yet unique boundary records.

java

Duplicate code

```java
public class MathOperations {
    int add(int a, int b) {
        return a + b;
    }

    twofold add(double a, twofold b) {
        return a + b;
    }
}
```

Strategy Superseding: Giving a particular execution to a strategy in a subclass.

java

Duplicate code

```java
public class Creature {
   void makeSound() {
     System.out.println("Some conventional sound");
   }
}
```

```java
public class Canine expands Creature {
   // Strategy abrogating
   void makeSound() {
     System.out.println("Woof! Woof!");
   }
}
```

9. Utilizing Connection points:

Classes are bound by a contract when they implement interfaces.

A class can execute different points of interaction.
java
Duplicate code

```java
// Interface
public point of interaction Shape {
    twofold calculateArea();
}

// Class executing the point of interaction
public class Circle executes Shape {
    twofold span;

    // Constructor
    public Circle(double range) {
        this.radius = range;
    }

    // Carrying out the connection point strategy
    @Supersede
    public twofold calculateArea() {
```

bring Math back. PI * span * range;

The Bottom Line:

Objects typify information and conduct, and classes characterize their design.

Constructors introduce object state, and strategies characterize object conduct.

Polymorphism allows method overloading and overriding, whereas inheritance makes it possible to reuse code.

Interfaces characterize contracts for classes to execute.

Day 4: Added Java Thoughts:
Welcome to Day 4 of your Java learning adventure! Today, we'll take a gander at likewise made contemplations that will moreover encourage how you could decipher Java programming. Might we anytime plunge into subjects like novel case making due, document I/O, generics, and hanging.

11. Intriguing case Making due:

11.1 Endeavor Catch Blocks:

Exception overseeing is fundamental for coordinating fumbles that can occur during program execution.

The endeavor get block grants you to supervise exceptional cases easily.

java Copy public class ExceptionHandlingExample's code;

attempt; Code that is capable of throwing an exceptional case int result = divide(10, 0); public static void main(String[] args);//

System.out.println("Result: " + result);

// Managing the special case System.out.println("Error:");   get (ArithmeticException   e).   + e.getMessage());

    }
  }

```
  static int divide(int a, int b) {
    return a/b;
  }
}
```

11.2 Finally Block:

In the finally block, code that must be executed, regardless of whether an exception occurs, is executed.

java

Copy code

```java
public class FinallyBlockExample {

    endeavor {
        // Code that could throw a surprising case
        int result = divide(10, 2);
        System.out.println("Result:   "
+ result);
        get         (ArithmeticException
e)//Dealing with the special case
System.out.println("Error:    ").    +
e.getMessage());
    } finally {
        // Code in the finally block all
over executes
        System.out.println("Finally
block executed.");
    }
  }

  static int divide(int a, int b) {
    return a/b;
  }
```

```
}
```

12. Record I/O:

12.1 Examining from a Record:

Java provides classes like FileInputStream and BufferedReader for reading from a file.

java
Copy code

```java
public class ReadFromFileExample {

    attempt (BufferedReader peruser = new BufferedReader(new FileReader("example.txt"))) {
        String line;
        while ((line = reader.readLine()) ! = invalid) {
            System.out.println(line);
        }
    } get (IOException e) {
```

```java
        System.out.println("Error reviewing from the account: " + e.getMessage());
```

12.2 Relationship with a Record:

You can use classes like FileOutputStream and BufferedWriter to keep in touch with a record.

java

Copy code

```java
 BufferedWriter;
IOException;

public class WriteToFileExample {

    endeavor (BufferedWriter writer = new BufferedWriter(new FileWriter("output.txt"))) {
        writer.write("Hello, world!");
    } get (IOException e) {
```

```java
        System.out.println("Error
staying in contact with the record: "
+ e.getMessage());
    }
  }
}
```

13. Generics:

13.1 Prologue to Generics:

You can make classes, coordinated effort imprints, and methodology with type restrictions utilizing generics.

They give type security and enable you to approach more adaptable and reusable code.

```java
java Duplicate code//Nonexclusive
class Box> private T content;

    public      void      addContent(T
content) {
        this.content = content;
```

use public T getContent() to retrieve content;
    }
}

13.2 Using Generics:

You can use generics with various data plans and classes.

java

Copy code

```java
public class GenericsExample {

    Box<String> stringBox = new Box<>();
    stringBox.addContent("Hello, Generics!");

    Box<Integer> intBox = new Box<>();
    intBox.addContent(42);

    System.out.println("String content: " + stringBox.getContent());
```

```
    System.out.println("Integer
content: " + getContent() intBox);
  }
}
```

14. Threading:

14.1 Preface to Strings:

Strings contemplate synchronous execution in Java.

The String class can be expanded, or the Runnable spot of cooperation ought to be conceivable.

java

Copy code

```
public class MyThread creates String {
  public void run() {
    for (int I = 0; i < 5;
System.out.println("Worth" + "I" +
Thread.currentThread().getId());
i++)
  }
}
```

```java
}

public class ThreadExample {

    MyThread     t1     =     new MyThread();
    t1.start();

    MyThread     t2     =     new MyThread();
    t2.start();
```

14.2 Connection Point that Can Be Run:

A substitute method for making strings is to utilize the Runnable affiliation point.

java Execute Runnable for (int I = 0;) by copying the public void run() of the public class MyRunnable. i < 5; i++) {

System.out.println(Thread.currentThread().getId() + " Worth " + I);

```
      }
    }
}
```

Public.

Day 5: Taking care of records and performing input/yield (I/O) activities:

This is Day 5 of your Java planning! Today, we'll go over Java's record the executives and info/yield (I/O) capabilities more meticulously. Reading and writing to archives are essential skills for some applications. We ought to research different parts of record the board.

15. Record Overseeing and I/O:

15.1 Examining a Document:

Java provides classes like FileInputStream and BufferedReader for reading from a file.

java

Copy code

```java
BufferedReader;

FileReader;

IOException;


public class ReadFromFileExample
{
    public static void main(String[]
args) {

        attempt (BufferedReader
peruser = new BufferedReader(new
FileReader("example.txt"))) {

            String line;

            while ((line =
reader.readLine()) ! = invalid) {

                System.out.println(line);

            }

        } get (IOException e) {
```

```java
        System.out.println("Error reviewing from the account: " + e.getMessage());
```

15.2 Adding Design to a Report:

You can use classes like FileOutputStream and BufferedWriter to keep in touch with a record.

java

Copy code

```java
 BufferedWriter;

 FileWriter;

 IOException;


public class WriteToFileExample {

   public static void main(String[] args) {
```

```java
endeavor (BufferedWriter writer = new BufferedWriter(new FileWriter("output.txt"))) {

    writer.write("Hello, world!");

} get (IOException e) {

    System.out.println("Error staying in contact with the record: " + e.getMessage());
```

15.3 Analyzing Equal Data and Expounding On It:

There are two decisions while working with double information: FileInputStream and FileOutputStream.

java

Copy code

```java
FileInputStream;

FileOutputStream;
```

```java
 IOException;


public static void main(String[]
args) public class
BinaryFileExample try
(FileInputStream input = new
FileInputStream("input.bin");

        FileOutputStream yield =
new
FileOutputStream("output.bin")) {


        // Checking out and making
byte by byte

        int byteData;

        while ((byteData =
input.read()) ! = -1)
output.write(byteData);
```

```
    System.out.println("Error
overseeing twofold records:"); get
(IOException e). + e.getMessage());
```

15.4 Completing Java NIO (New I/O):

Java NIO gives a more present day and adaptable method for performing I/O undertakings.

java

Copy code

```
 IOException;

import java.nio.file. Files;

import java.nio.file. Path;

import java.nio.file. Paths;

List;
```

```java
public static void main(String[]
args) public class NIOExample Way
filePath =
Paths.get("nio_example.txt");


    // Staying in contact with a
record using NIO

    endeavor {

    Files.write(filePath,
List.of("Hello", "Java", "NIO"));

    } get (IOException e) {

    System.out.println("Error
staying in contact with the record: "
+ e.getMessage());

    // Utilizing NIO to survey a
report: lines =
Files.readAllLines(filePath);
ListString>
```

```java
lines.forEach(System.out::println);

    "Error perusing from the
document:"; System.out.println get
(IOException e). + e.getMessage());

    }

  }

}
```

Frame:

Record overseeing and I/O assignments are essential for working with outside data.

Classes like FileInputStream, FileOutputStream, BufferedReader, and BufferedWriter are consistently used for record I/O.

Java NIO gives a more present day and adaptable procedure for supervising overseeing I/O tries.

Assess an assortment of record plans, work on investigating from and writing to reports, and find out about Java NIO's capacities. To the shock of no one, feel free to ask with regards to whether you have any requesting then again if there's a specific point you should jump into further!

Day 6: Multithreading

Welcome to Day 6 of your Java learning venture! Today, we'll investigate the captivating universe of multithreading in Java. Multithreading empowers a program to play out numerous undertakings simultaneously, making it more effective and responsive. We should plunge into the essentials of multithreading.

14. Multithreading in Java:

14.1 Prologue to Strings:

Strings consider simultaneous execution in Java.

The String class can be expanded, or the Runnable point of interaction can be carried out.

java

Duplicate code

```java
public class MyThread expands String {
  public void run() {
    for (int I = 0; i < 5;
System.out.println(Thread.currentT
hread().getId() + "Value" + i); i++)
    }
  }
}

public class ThreadExample {
  public static void main(String[]
args) {
    MyThread t1 = new
MyThread();
    t1.start();

    MyThread t2 = new
MyThread();
    t2.start();
  }
}
```

14.2 Executing Runnable Connection point:

On the other hand, you can carry out the Runnable point of interaction.

java Copy the public class MyRunnable's public void run() implementation of Runnable for (int i = 0; i < 5; System.out.println(Thread.currentThread().getId() + "Value" + i); i++)

```
    }
  }
}
```

```
public class RunnableExample {
  public static void main(String[] args) {
    String t1 = new Thread(new MyRunnable());
    t1.start();
```

```java
    String t2 = new Thread(new MyRunnable());
    t2.start();
  }
}
```

14.3 String Synchronization:

At the point when numerous strings access shared assets, synchronization is vital to keep away from information debasement.

java

Duplicate code

```java
class Counter {
  private int count = 0;

  // Synchronized strategy
  public synchronized void addition() {
    count++;
  }
```

```java
    public int getCount() {
      bring count back;
    }
}


public                                class
SynchronizationExample {
  public  static  void  main(String[]
args) {
    Counter = new Counter();

    // Making different strings that
increase the counter
    String t1 = new String(() - > {
      for (int I = 0; i < 1000; i++) {
        counter.increment();
      }
    });

    For (int i = 0;) Thread t2 = new
Thread(() -> i < 1000; i++) {
        counter.increment();
      }
```

```java
    });

    t1.start();
    t2.start();

    // Trust that strings will wrap up
    attempt {
      t1.join();
      t2.join();
    } get (InterruptedException e) {
      e.printStackTrace();
     System.out.println("Count:    ");
+ counter.getCount());
    }
}
```

14.4 String Pools:

String pools deal with a pool of specialist strings, which can be more productive than making another string for each errand.
java

Duplicate code

```
import                java.util.concurrent.
ExecutorService;
```

Java.util.concurrent is imported.

```
Executors;

public class ThreadPoolExample {
    public static void main(String[]
args) {
        executorService                 =
Executors.newFixedThreadPool(2);

        for (int I = 0; i < 5; i++) {
            Runnable laborer = new
MyRunnable();

executorService.execute(worker);
        }

        executorService.shutdown();
        while                        (!
executorService.isTerminated()) {
        }
```

```java
System.out.println("All assignments finished");
```

The Bottom Line:

Multithreading takes into consideration simultaneous execution of errands, further developing proficiency.

Strings can be made by expanding the String class or executing the Runnable point of interaction.

Synchronization is urgent when numerous strings access shared assets.

String pools can be utilized for proficient string the board.

Day 7: Java APIs and Systems

Welcome to Day 7 of your Java learning venture! Today, we'll investigate Java APIs (Application Programming Points of interaction) and systems. Moreover, we'll apply the information acquired all through the week to construct a little Java application.

Prologue to Java APIs:

1. Java APIs Outline:

Java APIs give a bunch of classes and points of interaction for normal programming undertakings.
Two generally utilized bundles are java.util and java.lang.

2. APIs that are often used:

java.util: consists of utility classes for date and time, collections, and other data structures.

java.lang: Contains major classes like Article, String, and essential information types.
Model utilizing java.util:

```java
Duplicate code
ArrayList;
List;

public class JavaUtilExample {
  public static void main(String[] args) {
    // Utilizing Rundown from java.util
    List<String> names = new ArrayList<>();
    names.add("Alice");
    names.add("Bob");
    names.add("Charlie");

    // Repeating through the rundown
```

```java
    for (String name : names) {
        System.out.println(name);
    }
  }
}
```

Prologue to Java Systems:

3. Outline of Famous Systems:

Spring Structure:

Extensive system for big business Java advancement.
Gives modules to reliance infusion, angle situated programming, information access, and that's just the beginning.
Hibernate:

Object-social planning (ORM) structure.
Works on data set associations by planning Java objects to information base tables.

4. Building a Straightforward Java Application:

We should construct a straightforward control center based address book application:

```java
Duplicate code
HashMap;
Map;
Scanner;

public class AddressBook {
    confidential Map<String, String> contacts;

    public AddressBook() {
        this.contacts = new HashMap<>();
    }

    public void addContact(String name, String phoneNumber) {
```

```java
    contacts.put(name, phoneNumber);
  return contacts.get(name); public String getPhoneNumber(String name);
  }

  public static void main(String[] args) {
    addressBook = new AddressBook();
    Scanner = new Scanner(System.in);

    while (valid) {
    System.out.println("1.   Add Contact");
    System.out.println("2. Contact Search");
    System.out.println("3. Exit");
    System.out.print("Enter your decision: ");
```

```java
        int          decision          = scanner.nextInt();

        switch (decision) {
            case 1:
                System.out.print("Enter name: ");
                String          name          = scanner.next();
                System.out.print("Enter telephone number: ");
                phoneNumber          = scanner.next() in string form;
                addContact(name, phoneNumber) to addressBook;

System.out.println("Contact   added successfully!");
                break;
            case 2:
                System.out.print("Enter name to look: ");
```

```java
        String searchName = scanner.next();
        String result = addressBook.getPhoneNumber(searchName);
        if (the result! = invalid) {

System.out.println("Phone number: " + result);
        if not, use System.out.println("Contact not found");
        }
    break;
    case 3:

System.out.println("Exiting the location book application. Goodbye!");
        System.exit(0);
    default:

System.out.println("Invalid
```

decision. Kindly enter a substantial option.");
```
        }
      }
    }
}
```
This basic location book application permits clients to add contacts and quest for telephone numbers.

Summary:

Java APIs give a bunch of classes and points of interaction for normal undertakings, with java.util and java.lang being ordinarily utilized. Spring and Hibernate, two well-known frameworks, provide options for enterprise development and database interactions.

Building a straightforward Java application supports the ideas advanced consistently.

www.ingramcontent.com/pod-product-compliance
Lightning Source LLC
Chambersburg PA
CBHW050034260726
48658CB00005B/1599